mudtrombones
knotted
in the spill

mudtrombones
knotted
in the spill

Neil Flory

ARTEIDOLIA
PRESSPRESSPRESSPRESSPRESS

New York

Special thanks to Down in the Dirt,
swifts & slows, Fleas on the Dog, Sleet,
& Eye on Life Magazine,
where some of these poems have
previously appeared.

ARTEIDOLIA PRESS
New York

arteidolia.com/arteidolia-press

First Edition
Library of Congress Control Number: 2022923144
ISBN: 978-1-7369983-7-3

for Elaine, whose transformative love makes all my poems possible

poetrypoemspoemspoetry

beansproutgrasses

he st

      arts the riding lawnmower but quickful learn it turns tangled
up in tonguetendril languid beansproutgrasses of regret forget the/and
flippant. can't bend, the every spikefield of interstate milemarkers to
heel and dogma fists hitting vacuum space where windshield once soon
was. well, dismay bleats he sta

     rts it up again yes the billowing roar but turns to roil but swallows
whole the springblue cloud-scarred firmament and every onionpeel
mistake shivering off our tender dripping core so startled like wilting
prey beneath. these engines drop fil

thy little sodacrackers all over the concrete and foolhardy
toiletbowls/once draining kelp and crankshaftoil and lakebasins by the
dozen against every apprehension's time. he env

         isions the judge thus bellowing all night into
garbagecan tunnelvisions beneath the ash city of cracked streetcorners
obsessions and discarded rubberbands. he inv

     estigates the blade but no, it's still egregious grease
claiming twice uncertainties and deliberations on into all ragged
flickering points more westful than every vast acknowledged
perception. his fixless suddenly, intuition snap

        ping clean steeringwheel sparkplugs battery all
tumblingscreaming teakettle out to cliffs and sea while the wind points
and mocks an acid jig, but already against isn't doubts/reversals his face
has carved a paintbrush sketching an overturned boat polishing an
outoftune mandolin nudging a forest drained of need con

         fronting a longribbon lake churning with
any urgency but that for the next and fashionable useless
                 language

we'd be

            otherwise clientele
wow   thatsahugeribbon   singular

     truckload   of coarsecoarse dirt   dumped
headlongcrash flailingspill   into surgingriver well past
  panic makes no difference to the rage, bottles nothing thousandmile
silken/iron snaketrack through   resistant atmosphere
unmanipulate,
     diverted   by not knowledge, word, barrier

handsoff   freestylespin   or static   be
   convince nothing

streetmerchants   yell incessant
      for unanticipated vigor hey there's a throwawaywalnut
        under that oldwoodchip, however the ragged grass
offers some alternativegesture   or another,   yet couldn't buryfill
    intertwine of

sigh   couldn't thought we'd be
           roughandsmackedawake
all again in the city's strange tempest

fourdepartmentstores   yield   remaining only the products
of can't-look-beyond   absence

    then we might

knotted

crass garage
crater fixate
spool
splattering spackle stammering
                four thousand grackles
(instantaneously)

            whisper (not a

                  chance, they're not capable) (hey
                  just because you've never
heard it doesn't render it inconceivable, what of their relief) oh, what

a rift/   what a gash
              what a jawdrop ridiculous
ravine cakefrosting
paintpeeling crescentwrench countless
leaves tremble legions of metropolitan desks applaud
   the general pervasive intoxicating candlewax cacophony screams full
fortissimo dissonance in blazing passion-cannons of joy/JOY (just

because it obliterates
        the schoolmaster's rust-wheezing
        paradigm of joy doesn't mean
        it's not)

cornstalks

government buildings etc and the little hardware store
across the street. debris muttering through corrugated
steel. i stared empty eye empty eye wordless pulsating
residual they went about advancing advancing with
nothing sustaining silk of my rancid silence. but the
eye's blink and she reduced me forcefully into warm
slovenly syrup with a single swing of her long rusted
shovel, i collapsed oozed into wet slop filth slop filth
splattered all over the sidewalk helplessly getting mixed
up in horse manure the boots of businessmen old gum
wrappers cigarette butts etc etc etc etc etc splattered.
the fish market's towering rationalizations. projectile,
i resolved into furious blasting propelling etc etc full
velocity out into the surrounding countryside fields where
the old man with eyes closed dancing feverishly chanting
swinging a golden sword through the clear morning air
so clear of his visions explosive visions hallucinating
tempestuous dragons shapeless calamities fast approaching
approaching the villagers whispered snickered etc etc
etc of his daily escapades and i hastily adopted the form
of a few cornstalks for lack of a singular profound plan
hoping he wouldn't chop me to feeble ribbons in his utter
carelessness and persistent lack of attention to any and
all details. i leaned further. the dwindling afternoon
gagged itself. by and eventual by the village found the
slide to the ringing south. holes, a few pieces of ginseng
on the wind. termites.

aria

      aria zenith
    (and the audience: ah) the world
before this one so honey-sweet
intoxicating vibes in cool summer amber of
embellishing Time so easily meandering
        so benevolent flow the by and by
to bend is (always relevant)
(misconception: aria's nadir, impediment) but
          the moon's a true precedent
           its harmonies
evident for any adventurer willing
to chance the shortened limbs to climb
straight up off this futile earth, so mute
     so heavy
      and blind

The Thousand Crows

shut up you stupid idiots you imbeciles just look what you've done just shut up shut up right now she shrieked at the thousand crows scattered about on the bare brown earth beneath the shattered silver sky hanging in forlorn pieces scattered about in so many weary splintered pieces but they paid no heed just kept screaming and screaming caw caw caw caw caw caw caw caw caw caw caw until the distant wandering trees began to gather again their many fallen leaves caw until tiny rivulets from everywhere began to pierce and split the surrendering dirt caw caw caw until the liberating thunder seemed inevitable until the sudden wind returned in howling triumphant velocity until the massive golden flashes overhead (now undeniable) announced a new electric sky about to form

process

an ill-formed thought
      ferreting
      itself
      out
pointing its finger at the mirror
                  swallowing
          a cyanide pill
the sturdy,
      well-developed thoughts
      now advancing
               stepping over
               the body

Brass

a yellow/orange cat named Florida you know like the land of the
glittering orange groves wasn't it doldrums of that time in Florida
when I couldn't stand up on my skis and the boat dragged me such
lamentation through the river for seemed like six hours maybe a week
or something akin full bland blah of a doldrum afternoon and we drove
around around the falling-down seen-better-days town listening to free
jazz at top volume brazenly confronting one metaphysical
contradiction after another with brassy dissonant non-syllogisms of the
kind you just unleash wild and snarling right in the middle of the
major main-drag intersection man look how they just rip everyone's
tires to flailing ribbons yank axles clean off in mid-turn clatter clang
slambam like demolition-derby pandemonium oh but look out for the
hidden pathways of pervasive black cats in these pock-marked
backstreets around every turn seemed like yellow/orange/brass
emergency of a new ontological conundrum leaping out and the streets
went on forever ever ever ever ever ever ever ever ever ever ever
ever ever ever ever ever ever ever oh but so much weary wane after a
time wane/diminuendo strength of dissonance fading to warmer hues
of chalumeau clarinets and gentle subtones what were the clashing
chords anyway what's that chart wait but then *snap* my skis caught the
right resistance I jolted upright standing bold and brave and whipping
wet speed howling otherworldly *yaaaaaaaaaaaaaaaaaaaaaaaaaaaaaaaaaa*
and five seconds seemed like seven lifetimes of brazen blasting
unbridled fresh-off-the-vine euphoria

dirigible

      possible   of
the three-quarter
                          moon cloud-
choked version of
                              night
sky ash-streaked reinforced
   steel dirigible crawling across eventual of
                      surveying the
   too-far-slipping-down-into-   sludge
world
                          model
  of such derision indifferent
                  eventful impervious
to their stupid
                 factory pollutants of
  discontent the flailing
anti-aircraft fire bitter curses of
                    cynical
villagers
        lingering
smoke-hovering potentials
            in such dim
   concentrating compressing light
  of
    their
                   little candles

Pools

no no wait it's still too new it's unformed it's still just a blob
a fat smudge I need time to think to ponder to consider oh now
that's very interesting indeed you're saying if I just throw
myself into the pool of sticky antonyms well OK here we go let's
rock and roll let's ride what's the worst that can happen maybe
they'll ruthlessly kick me out of the High and Mighty Academy
of the Proper Poets oh wait I was never a member anyway so
who cares once upon a time in the translucent quiet of the
post-reason age after the old logic had long ago run aground gone
awry like the rusty derelict ship in the bramble-choked river
I was eating a ham on rye contemplating that sweet by and by when
the cat took a crap on the kitchen floor with seemingly a gleam
of mischief (or incoherence?) in her eye well I can tell you nothing
changed smokestacks still filled the sky flies still made those
faint and easily forgotten sounds in the tide of the prominent
discord suddenly the pale green jade hula dancer strapped to my
dashboard became so very distraught that she cried and cried
and fell face down and writhed and sighed in that juicy orange
pool of her own unbridled regrets and two doors down someone
sang fa la la la and next door someone sang do re mi while the phone
rang and rang and grieved and rang and finally committed suicide do
re mi do re mi and I tried to sing re a drop of golden sun but instead
my lips formed what I seem to remember as some sort of question
no specific details come to mind right now just something about
what particular incoherent storms of discord might engulf us come
the morning

Strength

we the rebels lost and losing
the eye of the hawk is keenly aware time crawls
in this room the air itself
crawls with a sort of hidden vipers
and oh I've seen the wild
trees we the rebels pledge we pledge
our allegiance we the converted administrators tenants of
defenders of step through
the trees into wide landscapes
of sun and no winter the box has no time
its sides so clearly drawn and oh the wild
fantastic trees swinging
wide across valleys in the land of the dance
of ultimate succulent bounty we the defenders
of boxes of the Great Machine but
what dreams dissolved there in the desert of transition
in the verses of that pledge but just imagine where
reaching out might find the voice bellows down
corridors the voice takes form behind you the leviathan
ride the leviathan of your yet music
oh I've seen great hawks soaring above mountains
and oh imagination true identity bursting out
screaming at us slapping faces
you can't point it out there will
be no impeachments here said
the young constricted man garbled
an exploration of poetry may be an affirmation
oh the fantasies of old
Tennyson's old strength that moved earth and Heaven oh I sit
in a comfortable chair again in this room
and the clock hums and crawls and
contemplates death
imagine a landscape of flesh and pure determination and
pure decay but decay is the toy for our
amusement what dreams may yet live as the
clock dies and the room holds fast it is our
greatest and most precious power and
Tennyson recognized our identity Whitman struggled
against great odds Camus knew well
the endless summer that ultimate joy has
no consequences and in the next life soon somewhere
I will truly be a hawk

cleave

        perception in luminous exposition, rusted
shipyard retreat the crashcourse shirleytemple albeit
          evidently moustache gas-filament wheezeheat
mechanism
        against garbagegoblet torque-rake against
        the chisel stenchtrumpet crankshafts late
in the visceral simultaneity impetus pistonwill javelin shrill
 of gyrate
      derive sweat curse eat cling perceive sharpbelieve the spiny
weedstrangled mudtrombones turned blasting BOILING BOIL every
          rollicking stickydrippy breakneck moment
of the greasefire morning into BEHOLD such the sharpening
ooeygooey raw resolute solidity

            passionsauce/   (vs.)
inevitability
  stuntdoubles
 the allovercrusted fussbudget

isthmus tourniquet

                                                        wing the vivid
trills turns bright ornamental flourishes fantastic modulations
fandango/shrill along the shimmering wavelengths of magnesium
slophouses clustering wrinkled far through the forlorn suppositions,
the tattered

                    paragons asking what of the seemingly speaking
vinegar mesh past candor din centering conscious cavity aggregates, all
in faltered will pale/shivering on what almost skin-solstice proclaimed
the mastodon's reefs and ridges; these stammering ashvoices flag the
clattering algorithms of every birch and piston, crank

                        the unbending otherwise into immediate
facades of dawnclipping turnstiles, iconoclast rhapsodies mend against
windmill machinations of these unanticipated airslabs forcing
chalk-choking corridors nonetheless as the ancient insects dancing
vivace agitations indeed accelerando slap-rituals on emerging
dissonance-crests under graying star-splatterings; cobblestones crumble
as luminous algae-coated oyster-visions leap forth rush blast of smoke
spray vibrant geyser-particles while exponential chromatic sunlight
proves the grim prediction shade-subtle far exhausting more elusive
than moonflashed intoxicating elixirs born in eyewaste of distant
swamptemples facing fine taffeta shockwave glancing on the
impossible perceptions isorhythmic understructures confluence of
portents and beacons distant these relegate such scordatura timelines
under pregnant fusion of crust-fracturing reservoirs, bacchanal searing
over

        endless dog day contingencies and once after the rift-varnishing
magnitudes of towering tessitura breakwaters and altissimo
convolutions breathless, but we could not envelop we could not

                                                    reconcile
encompass engulf awakening razor-perched out on the edge of the
torrential windswept field attuned fully to the incantations drifting
over the flickering ignition landscape of twisting power stations
precarious tents trucks corn harbored intentions miscalculations oh
and what seasons-thick unconceived stances might yet adorn/speckle
our blaze-emerging languages, what exhaust fumes might circle our
scarred ankles in the toxic armpits of rust-drowning filth-belching
factories, what crankshafts would sour worn and flailing snap under

vast weed-vomits of fissures fed through constantly born decidedly
denied extended vociferous jetfuel slits lethargic mildew crackling
cantilevers, propping up the quivering dam holding back the snarling
river even just for a few seconds or cardboard ragged lifetimes
secondary stuffed ratcheted into the broom closet of slopmop
ambitions clothesline tourniquet bias pretense harbinger
matriculations on the mudshelter mussels mannequins cracking on the
tilebones and scintillating elisions gave way to such claustrophobic
anti-affirmations burst climb stultify the territory out lastly yet we can't

      intimate the conclusion correct the follicle courses right
down to eventual subterranean drainpipes, acknowledge rooftops
outstretched crutching shriek fracture of the farthest dim capitulating
shrugs indifference swimming the ink-worn sidewalks down into
swampy promises essences amphitheaters of wordless humid
breath-suspensions intertwining fortunate anyway into unfurling
amber of the makeshift nevertheless, sweltering at last into this of the
unforeseen relinquish resign, all

in finally
till the winnowing
till the lifedawns
till
the milky vaporous
next
narrowing

of remarkable first
         silverflash

(sticks)

whipped wear worn weathered withered we
burned far long smoldering into flat the faded
painting bland stick figures lost of long coping
of flat tongues eyes scorched beards
unmotion of stopped on the dusty wall under
weak exhausted light-flicker (absurdity
giggles hiding his matchbox again in the old
chest of drawers) why yes there's a crackle
and hiss of new flame somewhere but I don't
think it's in this corridor, perhaps way off in
those cavernous chambers of the old north
wing, perhaps

of

sting of alcohol/the blood's ultimate depth. we've
performed this surgery time and times we botched the
faulty count of. don't forget the gloves don't forget
the arrogant spire that loves to forget its concrete supports
that laughs raw in retort ridicule above the apprehended
city all in the sprawling the stumbling under the
crumbling of.

I treated a wound of my own. silo, the clock the clock
screaming incessantly all around everything bitter
acidic drainpipe down into its absence of. inferno/alcohol
the cut's all formed kiln of river through a rainforest blazing
burst-tail of comet bullet learning all our formidable idiosyncrasies
across a tattered night sky ever emerging under the larger
neon banner the ringing resounding presence of. blood-chant
of wounds amidst utterly becoming amidst charred migrations
of nomadic river-reed worlds down silken trade routes of
presence/half-glow/abrupt tire-streak swerving into the
ditch/alley/drainpipe all interlocking the redundant absence
of. how long has this parking lot sprawled here? we
could find no trace on the pavement. admit stadiums of
failure, all our magnifications. slow distillation into new
lamplight of deeper appreciation and you realize that we've
performed all the seasonal round-dances, the surgical cycle
and cycle. eat some black-eyed peas for luck.

I dressed a wound of my own in suits of fine silk steel
shield against the raw flagrant impact of front-line
bone-straining metal scraping on wood on rock on muscle
fire-cleanse the rupture of. a year emerges juicy flailing
screaming from the womb the clock still screaming fleeing the
pulsating delivery room vowing soon it's just begun it's
bound to run its course of course because concrete's always
wet until it hardens brittle cracks shards useless to the pure air
stagnant unto another morning haven't we heard and heard the
remembrance of. I'm doing the inside whisper-speech of
botching faulty all the self-justifications. Labrador glaciers
confess to the ravenous Atlantic.

yes, even the spire. inside, under such lamplight of the
sub-breath. it's the understanding of.

continents

Adonis adorned
Apollo burst through
the door flourishing a sword
of spinning lava laughin' like the whole
damn universe was a knee-slappin'
punchline yikes leaping over oceans like
they dribbled dripped like
teeny itsy bitsy weak little sad
forlorn forsaken creek-trickles
in woods way off the main
road of anything you ever ha ha
hahahahaha found the perennial
chuckle-fit about out there stomping
across the continents turning
over trash cans rolling up
wheat fields in giant eucalyptus
leaves and smoking them with haha
hooray firecracker mezzanine breakfasts
bursting with cakes and berries Adonis
cries out hey what
gives why isn't the camera pointed
at me ME alone because I
was promised something
like a measly paltry 15,000
years
of fame

flutes

well if you did decide to go
that way he said I think what
you'd want to do would be to take
these instruments
                    with you
                    handing
him four Geiger counters and a flute

uncomfortable proximity
of these ravines they mutter
   to themselves
       all night try shutting
your
         mouth in the interest of another
alternative perspective the old
                    man finally bellowed

sounds trailing
over the landscapes
always find
those struggling
to stay behind, or somehow
                         to leave the line

flutes
carved of animal
bones
    (long before) recorded time

resolution: not to flee
when again
the count revealed no reading
                         at all
he followed ten deep trenches
down at last
until the celebrating sea

the track

all on the old track but then it *cracked* chuckled
the slap-happy red-faced old man *went*
all to trash and uselessness yet once my slip forward *oh*
the muck but watching watching the
crack for sudden open thoroughfares wait the cypress
trees *it's the trees* stabbing upside down the egrets dancing
flailing frantic up (down) my nostrils the dank
algae-crusted tunnels to yawning caverns drill eleventh
reiteration into the soft core into
the other side of the,   *long-ago palaces*
                              once from the moment
                                        to come

little red flowers

ignoring no
wait appreciating   my leg itches
the half & half spilling all   scratch scratch not
down the side of the cup all over the counter   enough yet my
without differentiation spreading such glowing   just-waking-up eye
mess/love equal to all and the lake effect   itches scratch only amplifies
on-&-on snow not   ha remember that time at the Buffalo
differentiating street   airport no parking spaces anywhere not for one
from yard city from country from lake   desire/dollar or fifty no they
from rich poor wicked saintly well-   weren't my friends their talk
intentioned & negligent & ignorant in   and bluster all in time
equal glistening crisp distribution freeze-love   attenuated my glasses
over cars/trucks/motorcycles   need cleaning again no that
bald tires & new in equal slip/cling/claw   silly business has to wait
up the hillsides through the intersections of all our   until this coffee
wild contrasting interblending mess-passions/regrets   until all these
that we couldn't contain any longer   considerations William McKinley
that we couldn't procrastinate about   shot in Buffalo 1901 no love
until after we treated ourselves to day-old donuts   there but still that
& gallons of weak/cheap tea that fades even in the glass   didn't
fades even for the millionaire who'd   assassinate the zeitgeist's
never consider drinking it anyway   giddiness all spilling out of
                mouths/pens/printing presses/eyes everywhere onto
          the streets & hillsides William James on my white painted
     shelf ready to bring such of all that fabled/faulty/hollowed optimism
   now long assassinated by war/lies/our stubborn tendencies unburied
despite such
     equal passions/intentions/efforts of so many masses & then there's
        Williams Faulkner & Shakespeare right next door each with
     his own
       shining/straining/rickety/scarred/attenuated zeitgeist yet ready to
     burst all out again splattering onto
 either of my same-old dirty lenses as if nothing ever got buried after
all but no not now not until this I'm too busy too preoccupied
in this unmarked minute stirring in the sugar looking at the stained
ceiling procrastinating not grabbing
any napkins for the spill not hesitating in forgetting it
all now stumbling upon/finding the full blooming appreciating of those
little red flowers painted in a painted flea-market frame on this
painted red wall newly appreciating that
absolutely they don't droop/faint/alter/attenuate/fall into buried in the

unyielding freeze indeed they don't differentiate any eye
from another neither greed nor cowardice whatever vision functions
they greet and flourish in equal vivid vivid hues of five-and-dime
passion/sincerity why such joy of I could even take them off the wall
take them out on my cracked/weathered front
steps hold them high as a short arm's reach for
        anyone to see their amateur forthright bravery just for anyone
        anyone anyone anyone anyone anyone happening to drift by
all in an undifferentiated now on a nothing-unique-about-this street
that isn't closed on top of a hillside that isn't hidden that greets sun or
clouds or snow-buckets or engulfing nights all the
     same in-all-reality every calendarless equal-cycling hour of every
fully emerging falling-apart season/cycle/day

deadbolt

Thought of inch. But scorched, drowning in that gulf
between, each microscopic wave towering, stoic, power
of separation beyond all reckoning reach. Transformed
gaze in no form. Glimpsed mask. Fingertips slip,
dance momentarily in nothing, look about at painted
wastes with a shrug. Mirage? Series of sand-gulfs, each
choking further and complete than scoured ancestors
worlds long submerged. Inchoate dissonant throttled
interpretation yet managed amidst granite crashing of the
so utter NEXT, serving again for separation and stationary
relation lifeless faded plastic broken on soundless concrete.
Flailing reaction mischaracterized as calculation.
The rain continues. The forest, albeit in prime year's
green, has not moved. His shelter at the edge of it, near
the road. I suspect some invocation could be pronounced,
an unexplained intuition now lifting me into the
exotic light of that portal. Whine of trucks away on
other roads. The shining beetle, choosing to stay instead on
this side of the tiny twig. Every scorched inch once again
dissonant this soundless gulf. Closed and locked.

the gathered

the pecking order was established then
revisionist histories/symbologies/meditations
given out on the small flaps of matchboxes also
advertising cheeseburgers/brake jobs
also certain cards whose meanings at the time
seemed self-evident but later couldn't
be explained at all by either the headmaster
or the country doctor/musician but she stood back
now scratched her wrinkled chin eyed the
gathered lot decided yes to proclaim
to the audience view us carefully
only through the desolation/tranquility of your
magnificent souls but
know beyond a distant
doubt that no one
boasts the wisdom of the wind

salt-grains

                    fan-squeak
                            qkqkqkqkqkqkqkqkqk
    wheezewhine   sp spspspsputt er sputter sp sp spsp   hnhnhnhn
the tinygray   feather
    caught   in a downtown   sidewalkcrack   (grind) ndndndnd
                            hnhnhnhnhnhnhn
qkqk oblivious monotony of bootshoeshoebootshoeon on endless
tire-legions, their steel
        such willful the clenched indifferentntntntntntntndndndndnd hnhn
spspspsp wasn't nt   no]nd (ultimately the slivering similarity
        couldn't   ndndndndndthe state of things, ofthematter
thematter thematter crumbles   spsp   qk   ]nt
                into   vaporous, scissors scattering hnhn
the useless   ndndndndndndndnd
spspspsp   wavelengths   [qk   half-   expected
        towering inchoate silo of a (no
beyond)ndndnd(if it wasn't (after which the anchored momentarily
perhapshnhn vast   qk qk qkqkqk woundedlabyrinth spspsp   of this
    dustyalmostutterance dissolves, salt-grains   in Himalayan caverns,
the weatheredmudsplatteredsoul pressed   transparent, scrap hnhn
    qkqkqk sp   sp[of tissuepaper caught
on a warehouse roof in   cold rain,   qk qk   qkqkqkqkqk   ndnd
    qk[whiteout   forcetotality   enmeshedthese feeble   words
engulfed   ndndndndnd   hnhnhnhnhnhn   qkqk
inleathertwisted condemnation of
        theveryair   (O would that it still the)qkqk spsp   nd ndndnd
can't   ]nd   didn'tntntntntntntntntntntntntntntntntntntntntnt isn't
    ]nt   of the jackhammer diatribes drown   such a ritualheavy
        spsp sp   sp[hn]   continent his shouts
choked hnhnhnhn qkqkqk by vomitsurgesplattering   ndndndndnd
            the pavement [sp   hnhn   [nt
    shrieks   in hellbent proteststststststststststststststststststststststst
    even ndndndndndndndnd   (isn't) (where   (nearly   (soon
theveryunderpinnings of   spspsp sp sp sp ndndndndndnd
    charredlanguage qk qkqksp sp spspsp ntnt coastlines   ]qk nd] nt]
shrinknknknknknknknknknk sink
                    sinkweight of certain   qk   ]qkqk   hn]
loss ndndndnd(weight)ntntntntntntntntthe forgotten   spsp
            exponential essence-emptied stststststststststst
taking   hold further   by allandplentiful   ndndndndnd qk

/quickthe accelerating///////////////breakneckblankdrawing
gouged-out
seconds   (and no you cannot say)ndndndndqkqkqk qk qk   spsp
hnhnhnhnhnhnhnhnhnhnhnhnhnhnhnhnhnhn

mountainside

we'll figure it out
said the derelict philosopher on
the barren winter mountainside to
the hyperactive cricket singin' laughin'
JUMP and jump again all my friends
to the true barndance tune of all
time vivace allegro presto in golden
haste yes truth-time in the shining
thread weavin' its way through and
past this blessed day and we hasten
to wait accepted fate and in such lovely
idle haste not a thing but to always
sing no wait shouted the old man as
an avalanche of a thousand old and
cantankerous syllogisms overwhelmed
him again

window

many roads,
        mostly the flow

Memory, her woven eyes of neon beacons in haze,
     fine multitude dream-threads until silken pure resonance
the gaps, lodged far immersion alluring
        black questions, spun texture among leisure
   expensive rare caress, slip and constant the flow

mostly the air in haste past my window, my hairs
  imperceptibly disturbed, separated
          each in full glide exactly the pathways will
       the expensive inescapable Becoming

her woven dream

King of Clubs

                      auxiliary switchback, reciprocating
addendum to the intermixture switcharoo nightshade past
precocious such all plastering King of Clubs, his sword flimsy
syrup plop plop dropdrip in the sewerpuddle cracked curb stormdrain
snickerbeetle cling/ and again such pencils and wondrous almanac
scar-ballads splashing forth dribble glee along the burningpinkish
flabbergasted bright boulevards, the cafes exploding teeming
festivals of vainglorious and evanescent, sundry till sundry/after/
sundry glib lip anchor freeze/thaw out after/the neversurprise
process, uncease

slammed
satiated your tarnished muscles
force hard against the frictionvent while dust-choking bricks bellowed
haggard at the splintering disintegrating east flickering aloof
to partitions corrugate still the excessgallon obfuscate, oh fickle
fickle imprint faint, what daguerreotype fingerslipped till buried in the
old-century dry dregs, couldn't latch/the filter
the filter

                    man can't you finetooth comb can't it all sift
sift sift scrape the wildly rich glissando resonant membrane wet
riverpebbles sawdust clay particles of stained plastic scraps of ragged
burlap oregano pinches full knotted to fine vapors and
half-remembered ultimately futile non-referential conjecturings

yeah gotta know gotta perceive
all manner of shout chantcry bustin' the tattered stitch like overloaded
cargo ships on slathered slats of sanctimonious grease, but consider
that sameold sawdust mutterings after decay residue at last invents
piles piles of derelict contaminated skyscrapers isn't really the usual
conspiracy in the eventual slightest, not at all good citizens and
proprietors and gracenote dimestore turn-on-a-dime smalltime
scrappysharp volunteers, good
magistrates and seaborne soothsayers

communication

for maybe a cheap thrill anything the sun
the tyrant in boasting in anger frozen in
his far northern castle he exclaims
waiting for wisdom in circles
garbled she said all our world is fragments our thoughts
are clusterings fragments and all
confusion our thoughts static condensations
of mud dry lifeless
mud cracking in the merciless heat this team is a non-solution beyond
the mountains and the plains he shouts blank
both staring long each waiting for
perhaps truth or even some welcome
comedy or a cheap insult to spew wildly from the mouth
of the other but there is just nothing the utter
void cheap unsalted
cheddar insults usurping their unsettled
cool confident cowardice garbled we
have failed i love the idea
of wisdom exclaims the professor in his cold room
i love books truth beauty and the quest for wisdom but we
know all he really loves is his secret
fear and the quest for tenure hey what say we go
grab a burger she said communication
fails garbled failure abort distort
static sta   tic
the lines are cut and he said i don't care
where we park just anywhere that team doesn't work the
large ship
flounders so they drove around and around the
town in jokes in freedom
in joy in noise he said oh suddenly i
am so profoundly depressed i could just hurl the sun like boasting Zeus
hurling down spears of great violence abundance
and passion then the wind
whipped up wild in great strong gusts tumbleweeds
dissolved dust danced thick in miniature swirling tornados
and laughing for a moment she thought
she heard his voice laughing just before the wind
whisked his words away into
nothingness saying life
is one big damn glorious
and most incredible improvised

solo

Outstretched

in contradictory phases opinions on the slopes of the dirty
hill beneath that great philosophical mountain they clash
and scrape shift shift to one side or the left sleeve down that
sleeve they always turn oh darn it it's really it's finally a really
messy irrational place after all isn't it it is it tells the
controversy the unexpected posturing of phony philosophers
seabirds bathing in a parking-lot puddle near the skatepark an
exhausted middle-aged man unshaven fearful walking slowly
past an old leaning wooden fence the paint chipped piles
of particles of forlorn green existences questioned contrary the
contrary always the otherworldly grace or mess of that extra
vision toss it to the wind it flies easily and true well now I tell ya
we've all got our flights of fancy take it take my damn worthless
money all my two-bit junk but you'll never take away my
orange eagle with the fiery breast I'll jump right on his titanium
back frolic in a laughing-eyebrow sky of time suspended denied
those benevolent fantastic wings stretching wild no quantity
from one burning horizon to the other

Ruins

,if not. ,ultimately insensitive; still monuments purchased amidst environments charged full with forebodings and consequence, crippled unvoice stark rush of thick dunes trampled on stretching long and blending harsh dissonance into distance, flagrant conglomerations yet into what vivid shatterings unfurled under once that true impending explosion of solar fury?

There were runners in the ruins, their silhouettes flickering erratically between the shifting shadows, until at last engulfed in shadow, neither to emerge again in this hour or the next. Hilarious calamity incessantly tangled tight through ultimately indecision trilling shrill vociferous against unperceived frigid clarity in all rotting ravenous Rust, the gates disgraced, awkwardly ajar until all these schemes and final misanthropes come just to mud-rivers drowning the fields their spent expanse, their doldrums and exhaustions blazing in agonizing depths of August. Vast, barren, wind-scorched into what fabled and romanticized beyond, the raging tornado snapped his matchstick legs! We bided our time, at last content to run thrice and life-weary upon the inevitability of all this charcoal gilded Nothing come full and resonant home to mark its wind-swept signatures, even unto the definite resolution of long-coveted lore and all such questionable whispers. Pre-dawn gray; the sudden soul-filling tranquility of the orchard under soft rain.

;not one could claim it! We stumbled amidst splintered desks, vivid jagged introspections lacerations of shatterings in the burned-out blasted shells of teetering skyscrapers, fractured into useless shards on white-hot glowing sword-points of merciless advancing mountains; torrents of immediacy, flames licked his eyeballs! Center of ritual; convergence of powers and truths, transitory precipice on the softly shimmering gossamer borders of true contemplation. Dripping rainforests. The ruins, ever in their coarse remains. Beckonings, constants of all such newfound voices, their exhausted earthen shells cast to sweeping winds and trackless other open fields unknown, unperceived; ,if possible, perhaps by slim margins;

turnchurn Rome in the rollingride

                    oh the minglemerryslide
      humid   languid
               late afternoon
and the window's light-shaft
      reveals
whizdoodle giggleride on the hayroll hahahahaha gotta be a million
dust particles all so luminous writhing slithering thrusting twisting
intertwining in every conceivable sexual position oh such sprayhose
flowerburst of the pinnacles the splashpeaks a mass euphoric ecstatic
dust-orgy in

      golden   mid-air   microcosm

lavaflavorfire of the surgebird splurge HAHAHAHAHAHA spot the
spanglespin vroom on the gluttonbutton boomdance and Mister
Chuckling Sun finally chiming in *let ancient Rome burn all tinglequake*
torchburst turnchurn in the envynoose because this management will
claim no ringrope rifleplight responsibility for the adult content of this
spontaneous slipwiggle gigglefilm oh love the loving minglemerryslide
churn turn ye Romans all in the balloonlight and
               such of
           the reeling
       rollingride

(balm)

O wild Dardanelles
   O thick tributaries capillaries bold
  christening seen in dim sunlight
through the smudge-caked window of fortune's pain
    fortune's breathless relief the whole world tucked
away in a bottle of aspirin in the old locked
   cabinet long abandoned at the end of
    the hall my own pain the persistent aches
  of all when oceans seem to fold in on themselves
roaring and fighting when kings masturbate for money
sport stardom when all the weary world sings out
    to the silver air of singular situations known only
  by an incredible
  possible few
       (tucked away in a bottle)

 yet it's still something
  still maybe an expression of something
however vague however impossibly
   intangible (weightless fine gossamer of
    something not known free out beyond
our own flat earth-edges, aches) well honestly at least
one thing's sure as the sunset it's no doubt
    a whole lot better than just that pure thick
   dead silence
     known only, of course, by the dead

comprehension

yeah comprehension's a downright incomprehensible

                                     fool
lookathim all workedup all tiedupinknots tryin
tryin tryin tryin tryin squeeze sweat pull heave
bleed tryin but that hole's still just
a vast gaping
                     hole ,   whoa hey look   in there's New

Hampshire Saturn the Mariana Trench dull
pencils summer groundhogs fish tacos stained glass grief love
procrastination peonies sleet even an old man's next
                   little rinkydink
                            thought

chamber

(feels like) the high tide//////

(old complacencies collapsing in the
     under) edges/////until/----------threadbare

corner
                    /we're painted into

//stepping back into compromising
contingencies into improvising rapid-fire
contingencies collapsing again in the under
after edges edges after threadbare barren
edging into the stepping-back inches

/into   /windowless

nothing more

                    (save residue
/of squandering midnight)

trippingdown

                              (tinfoil airplanes falling
howling out of the ruptured sky onto convulsing fields of pretzeled
          pistons and turpentine suppositions) salivating
mudsplattered sandpaper
stammering gelatinous granite acid-eyed sapphire hysteria bluster
                              (clamp) ratchet the dent hibiscus
outburst of variegated every blistering heatstroke strawgrasping
seizure/   our stopgap lastditch rustflecking rhododendron
souls,
                farmorecomplex than some
concocted
monochromatic
cardboard cutout plastic pre-fab kinda sillygooey jibberish bit of/
        hang on/   weekold slop-fisted enginepile belch-rot
of Gibraltar-cut skewed boiling gossamer cherries/   catapult out
of wild surging coral-toothed trench-infested improbability-reefs
anyway what
wondrous rootedthing could you even breathesputter on the topic of
                    trippingdown the few river-crusted
        stairs in that (nailpolish limestone) flimflam sham of an origami
skyscraper   /hey
          whatweretheyevensaying   /what
/sock-stuffing tile-chipping dripsyllables sinew-knotted sauce witness
            scrapyard weeds otherworldly splintering floodgates hellbent
        on outrageous rippling
corrugated out   /blast, forget
/forget it uttercompletely, all of

(unravel) yes,

you know such effortless;
                the slipback breathing
                    engulfing explosion-vivid,   the moment's rich
                              currentdrinking   /deep resonant
                    idiom

the convex/
(the mesh)   summit ledge
                        luminous

(overt
the noonday blindingly)   ski-slope

ears

gloopish
muckly all chum-rancid
the self-kilned
        GARBAGE CANS of his
bugrotly ears and the same old big
dumb plastic grin all jeedleree SKLEE as
he *gladly oh so magnanimous* tips
        to one side inviting and so
as usual the beautiful blood-crimson
        butterfly
        vomits
all blishing quishly blooshingly slop
                        plop
                       down
into the crusted canal *slish/slock*
of spillage
on the chipping
        clipping
                hiffy/sliffy/pliggius tiles,
all the while
proclaiming herself to be
repeatedly repeatedly repeat after
me so you can be free merely
        a muted
        yellow
        hummingbird
all around the frosted cupcake tree and
all on the sweet *fleederee teedleheehee*
        sklee and skleederccceeee

was

melts.   sc   atters

                the want   was
                     mute   (fo   ssil)

thin
    air-imprint decreasingly
  depth filled flat far
                    blank   mesa   scoured
            tongueless
                        null   deaf

the shut   was   tatt   ers

    worn sp   lit threads   far lean-to
                                                    head
                                                    wind   clot
                            snap   null

lack   pickaxe splinter   the
                                    blunt lack
                    toothpick   the just was
                                        of this thin   sift
ago

one
sliver
crack, to slush rivulets open less this to renderless yes even
June's this amber mourn holding was
                            the reach
                                                    was

mute   of was   melts,   mesa's
                                            remnant   not
        if this flat once
                    the shut was
                    the want   thinning
                                                    was

i think we could be in the third quartet

eye thrown to some elsewhere the blink of a fractured moment i turned
the old knob just a half inch too far the wrong way no margin *thock*
roll it fell full on forceful floor in the pure dark on the other side of the
old door of the high room on the narrow long stair and i could do
nothing just such scrapings of nothing but she'd want you to try, right,
well yes even if just for the purposes of maintaining i washed the coffee
cup out again and again again again again still on full again gaze
through the same stain the same familiar brew ultimately sometimes it
seems a sense of stability but what exactly necessitates that do you
consider for instance isnt it from another perspective a pure hindrance
once a locked gate meant to replace that ancient doorknob years ago
but what distant point revisionist alternate rendition in its own sense of
removed time the desire thrown to of what scorned elsewhere of
diverted eye or motivation/line followed off you can just now sense it
the sonata seems in developing spinning out perpetual around us now i
think we could be in the second (traditionally slow) movement but
wait are there even really movements when the only movement in
perceived action is continuous constant concurrent contrapuntal in
control left to the instinct of indistinct inexpressible intangible fully
formed full on the front edge of the flying foam of the four friends
crammed into the front seat of 1:17 p.m. *flashing* aboard an ultimately
gray and misunderstood afternoon or 27:86 Greenwich time or
equatorial whatever polar calibrated thrice/split/zone/partition
fractured cracked splintered shattered scattered defunct timepiece you
fished flailing from the full foam of the chop the wailing drink the
camera thrown into such of drink the images stale broken ultimately
failed through attempting to harness that which cannot be ever
harnessed and it slips and slips and oozes by despite every tremendous
vociferous effort and it flows by through every fracture and flaw the
furniture exudes no music and they took to shouting no its *you* who
are found predictable and wanting and useless to the timbre of this
moment *its you who cant harmonize* between the resolute resounding
ramifications clear through to the surface and the distance i think we
could be in the third quartet now but wait what if the knob is beyond
repair if the double bar refuses in resolute rejection to ramble into the
scene of vignette of tableau of review of perceiving of suspicion of
conjecture of hypothesis of conspiracy of fantasy of old misunderstood
of tales spinning out perpetual around us now again the soap too much

swirled again again still on the once over and again covered over in the same faded stain the stair stops again at the door and nothing so much decided to find in it the ability the bold arrogance for the chance seeming change it was nothing scraped off the will of the thrown split/out/under/askance scar of stillness in second-chance sonatas in soliloquies in fractures found of havent these feeble chairs burst out off into arias again before the dusk fished itself out of that vast inchoate but wait i come to perceive it seems i believe they arent really harmonizing actually just bolted into sitting quiet still in no motion in no choices of motivation or inklings of twisted reaches of risking reactions opposite actions amidst the all fully spinning and slipping out from under around us truly again and all, elsewhere, opened, seemingly,   ,of again

ash

the smattering across (scrounging
bold impatience to free the bliss from
doldrums) a kiss against
the kettledrums' kick,
        he claims slick
        but not so cold

complaining counterweights
filter all the wishes' burdens yet
witness the magicians deny full province
        of the question/   musicians
mistaken for sages, complicit cogs
while chieftain's children feign
        golden elixirs, evident balms

but dusk's breath, he only intones
what's been carved
        and daily told

charleston in blue heather

        canyons in the ballroom banyans of the blossoming
canopy barnyard canaries barking at cars crashing blindly on the other
       side of the Hudson
        books on horticulture authored by collectives of Baltimore
housewives complaining about the hideous conditions of baker's
dozens bought with coins tarnished through heat of long summer cold
of belligerent
        winter brave colors bold colonels bursting into
        the clearing bright blue crows clawing at the broken
doors of cottages burned and collapsed in heaps of confusion
climbing bumblebees big carousels high-stakes carnival
        contests boardroom curmudgeons
howling crying in their burning hopes for blessed clairvoyancy
crystallization of halcyon dreams happy days are here huge craters
brimming with golden coins cash falling from the vast blue in heavy
blobs and clumps cracking buildings and bridges with their force a
bountiful harvest of
       hoarding
        hairy black caterpillars clinging to the barnacle crust the
broken hull of the capsized fishing boat battered blasted by hard surf
haughty boasting Congressmen calling out to mass of crowds hope
broad boulevards toward coping harbingers of
  happiness
     contentment close at hand checkered badgers blended colonial
hills into armored chests of captains held to
       duty and brethren cloaked hiding in blackness of
  unknown bonds the crimson cords color of blood hanging proudly in
secret halls castles overlooking forgotten harbors
       float
         in the transparent
green film flapping on the clothesline the jagged treeline etched high
across a giant mountain of slime filth decay generosity beneficial
       chances good cheer before we're
       captured finally engulfed in the sun's
flames well hello there happy happy California everyone look high
across the broad canyons behold the vast expanse of blue beyond so
       clean
       so completely clean and clear a few
steps to the left then to the right captivated by the music and the
carousel turns and turns and we hope against hope burn in combustion

of hope for some kind of comfort some simple morsel of consolation
perhaps in the form of a
                  bauble   or
                        heirloom or charming
                                      prize

edifice

rusted wrecking balls
Ideal's edifice smashed, strewn
across the wet cobblestones
vivid banners torn
from bricks, battered streetlamps,
trampled into forsaken
boulevards of dust   they
chained themselves to wishful
anachronisms of convenience,
sputtering machines of the
derelict factory, while   outside
the surrounding (rebuilt) city shines,
hums, forgets,
speeds on ahead

not the words

sudden VIOLENT
TILT
of the world

merciless,

gut-twisting,

angle

exponentially

extreme, cherished knowns

hurled tendon-snapping

vigor no hesitation into

sharp

variegated gelatin of uncertainty,

pestilent disbelief

all the little houses, so colorful

the impotent skyscrapers all

tumbling

so very d   d

o

w   o

n

w

n

those three shrieking in the scrape, shift

but he says nothing

dry coarse painted face of

stone

careening,

stoic

invasive crow

long has the putrid

knowledge of it nested

granite-heavy,

uninvited within him

but not the words,

elusive intonation,

enchanting

invocation

of a possibly theoretical

enveloping

equilibrium

spill

got junk bliss
junksketchy kitschbliss clip out the slipglue stopgap clamp seeming
ditchdirt split past the ragged one

          bet jagged
brokethrough bustlaugh shovedup glassdance slapdash crass/off
the fool flimsy designated pinch, got willing the vociferous hootenanny
fakeout and the colossal whatnot debris

        witness esteemed Cornelius
Smithson Jones, his skills to hone owning his corkscrew
truckloads   slack up the runt no to beguile
inflicting runtstack of stufftacks up the straight center of a backlog
brain, till Jones trashed lax epitome kink lumber clasp
the lackluster
hammerhandles   plastic flipgiddy flowchart
windfall
machinations, if/then rationale rinse the flightrisk taut climb clench
fistcramp lastditch throwaway
squeezedthrough
scroungedout slipscribble cobble makeshift
twine

        handmedown
inksplatter hit chunk the plank gaffe guffaw such swimsoupy rollicking
hootholler nonperceptions bleeding
into some sort of perhaps
patchedtogether solid iffy/something like

        flunk the lump
blot
stutter applause angle don't truncate the flirtatious
haggle of what you couldn't forgetfully filigree frame, sneaky Sullivan
oh twofaced sweat-glisten Sullivan

        nose the spiffy sputter
snifflenose ficklepicky shut blunt secondtime flunkedout crumbling
of the ceremonial basement
latch, taciturn   breaklace render spongekick
bristleclick the mister-slick-fool mumbledrama derelict gruntblister
fizzlecourse scorn of the scavenger
windbag brat, try out fast claptrap in the rancid gloaming
the scarred icedrifts

        ah yes again such thick headbrick
headstrong luckless mister Cornelius Jones, he tricked the kitschy

wishbone the sketchy worstcase wishbone into all sorts of horticulture
misconceptions,
all slices
of random rumored misdirections

dry

can't
divebomb
dessicate
some miasma goldrush
of flowerpickled
half-utterance simultaneity in kind
grifter
ringleader
regiment
overwrought
caisson
stenchbomb flailing
crashcourse of you'd
brazen
saltwater scrapegouge striation brazen
brazen makeshift of all
they
finally lilting mosaic
couldn't be

vs.

weldmeldn   ess
of dilettante
con   vexly honed   ]oriole
hey glib slim luckydice out
the fullness cavityesque   vs.
stark   \tonnage   of
                          isn't

]what we
/split   /heavy of   he
built   ]what we
leviathan   /clipped   ]forallintents
drainpipe of   ]andsoforth
out of hardscr   abble   \nail
tablescraps   /split   edge
vacant lot   ]ju   nkchoked
nowh   ere *can't*   \late
ast   oni   shment   iron
                          vs.

]vs.   spooling   \vs.
shyster vs. cod
liver vs. winter
waning erstwhile   ]divots
/split   vs.
trinketly   ]pinched
we   sp   entlikehell on
/floppy   whentrusted
on foolhardymeasures   ]nobreak
funnel   ]evcrylittlecoin
/bucklesunder   our   investdr   ip
squeezethatadrenaline   ]ha
sawthatedgebutdisregard   ha
frayblend spill   ]somanylittlepieces anklecut
clip twi   ceshy vs.
cantileverly and marshmallowreeds
                          sway

\acce   lerando   tallgrass
\behemoth   oh but heysport   ]just itchin swim
disregard cotton   ]candyexpandness (sotto
voce) stand *won't kneecap itself* yesterday
          and all aplenty

49

contain

little mouse-houses/
built in little darkened crevices
of these   cavernous
Northern houses
                but not

a word to claim/acknowledge/explain (hide
and seek?) spare me all games, just
let me be to drink my old tea in this parlor's
dim light, since despite any plight whatever
remains
or leaves a residue/stain strikes beyond
all pull of me and mice or lice
won't turn to grain and
                      yes
knowing utterly certainly that late-night rain
will always/only clothe itself
in sheets and robes and ribbons
                  of late-night rain

Act

why did the sunlight yell at me he wondered aloud who the hell
cares exclaimed the cracks in the sidewalk we've got enough of
our own problems trying to survive in this outrageously unstable
trash bin of a world so get the hell out of here move on down the
road buddy and don't step on any of us unless you want to break
someone's back and then a little green lizard walked across one of
the cracks but suddenly a stray cat ate the lizard but then a big
groundhog jumped out of the bushes tried to intimidate the cat
but the cat wasn't having any of it and then fiendishly flagrantly
snickering uncontrollably he stepped on a crack and the crack
yelled *OW STOP THAT THIS INSTANT* but didn't break anyone's
back hey cut me some slack shouted the sunlight I'm the one out
here every day trying to make this thing work like the magic
charm of the century and I called to the clouds five or six times
but they just ignored me the damn fools sliding off to choose some
other merriment over me and I gotta find a holiday gotta break out
of this circular grind I'm finding this ever ever-act of *filtering down
into all and everything* to be particularly tiresome and monotonous
at this point in time and why does it have to be everything anyway
and where are those clouds come back I'm sorry I called you
fools I didn't mean it you're all heroes and royalty of the earth come
back man can't wait till winter when I can finally take some
time off

cliffs

engine's
combustion
energy
after
filtered down
distilled   dust bits
of fertile earth smeared
pianissimo awareness of   her
ritardando   nostrils

bare boulders, fact
of
their
weight

gradual
floodwaters, their gray
patience,
         glass doors open let in all
debris stricken anthills
bleed industrious to paralysis
to
     crumble
he mumbles   something
        undecipherable

dog days
birdless   coastal cliffs
their fact
is its own weight

vivace vision claims
privilege decisive reach in sun-mesas but
then sharp *sforzando*
of his shattered knee no
run no return filthy tile-shards washed
away down sewer-streams to
hum
to stagnant

of late-days
              earthen dusks

of gravel
      in frigid light
               of fact

islands

these bright rainforest islands
    of jubilation in
  a wide river of mud/sludge/stink
or maybe
it's the islands that spew full putrid/stench
          while the river's wildly blindingly
          luminous all in a fantastic
joy-thing ringing singing flinging flowers and
party favors around everywhere ribbons and
bells bells *bells* all around the vociferous
sonority resonating chamber of the mind
flung open to air-flow free and fragrant
amidst infinite green distances light in
brilliance of otherworldly gold ringed in
leaping silver vibrance our
          perceptions the tentative
      step onto the ice-coated high wire
    between those two stoic skyscrapers
  emotional
       cargo ship listing this way
        or
        that
     any moment a rogue wave snap
of the fingers an affectionate
        purring
        house cat warm
bed inside a subzero night
or a sudden
     hurricane
          stamping its feet
out there on the seemingly
    snap-of-the-fingers
    here-or-there
horizon

lag

manifest
cellophane
ventricle
rivet
corrugate a
Polonaise flack
of all the subterranean
stuff & whatnot wanton
filthing past pesticide
out kitsch trills
and the spent sentient
folly
bag
tapdance
to strike that
zenithbalance resplendent but
resultant
only mire
in dumpstink
switchback
flat

Neon

all the coastlines in weird neon their magnificent stalactites in full
vibrating glow now motionless cautious awakening immediately from
remembrance of no dream and the traffic surging in red frenzy outside
the window the streets blazing electric gyrations and just at that
moment the music accelerated a grand fortissimo explosion frantic
fever pitch pulsating WILD pounding SLAM all around him bursting
through the door he runs like hell full tilt wide eyes clenched fists
flailing down the corridor SLAM through the opposite door out into
the darkened plaza joining thieves bankrupt stock brokers
disenchanted politicians howling down the caverns of empty office
buildings the clouded ravines of existential exaggerations when
evidence in the eventual rounding way of time and the misunderstood
breath of every moment would find one unquestionable artifact upon
the mantle the dashboard instruments all confused in the first
encounter they rejoiced claimed to be his kind yet when the moment
came they gave rejection without hesitation or apology shocked he
wandered yet soon solidified into no need for them a steadfast rejection
in turn soon took hold of distant cliffs in new streams of wind he
carves out a flat dry place stone-fisted fury of construction rope rivers
of cut lumber bricks ambition of muscle and sweat ambitions of
skyscrapers of maniacal ceaseless factories in the grinding dusk dust of
a hundred deceptions falling free off her heels striking resonant the
littered pavement gravel her furtive heels in haste he begins to sense the
limits of his drive drawn near finding oneself now in these frigid
borderlands toward a man unknown unimagined in this century
infantile erudition without obvious sense instinct machinations of
instinct marred by the passage whose flame flourished beyond all
anticipations that morning in the mountain pass the deep snow nearly
zero visibility for a time it seemed we'd never get out VIVID colors rich
bold environments every succulent wondrous detail in unbelievable
SHARP relief each pebble of a multitude brilliant in the sun each tiny
shadow carved of hard definition as crystal or shining granite and you
will not be static you will not remain the man you were inevitably you
will be transformed despite your most passionate efforts in
motionlessness out on the deck she turned to me laughing the sunset
behind her the spray in her hair singing what is life if we can have only
one what are dreams if we cannot cast them striving far out beyond
what all our eyes can see and they were talking under the leaves in the

waning afternoon and the older boy said to the younger if you do not bring forth the fire then the world will be without fire entirely destitute inconsolable a place of all barren and wanting the prince his hours so very precarious and volatile his name his blood worth far more than his ideas beliefs opinions you've got to be kidding convictions don't be ridiculous (a crescendo of laughter from the audience) but seriously folks we all know the designs in the minds of his siblings let's face it in certain environments perception weighs more than reality my father in extreme priceless wisdom said son in the everyday neon comedy/tragedy photoplay of that place it's not who you are but the role you're in that's important beautiful predictions yet disappointments discovered dilutions fragmentations unwanted adjustments to our course unexpected improvisations but what else are we to do when all of this comes down listen I'm sorry to disappoint you but there's no one here who knows the answers to your questions we don't know where all this leads or what the next hour holds all we know with any certainty is that we're doing our best it was twilight and just beginning to snow when he returned to the apartment a long month in pursuit of elusive diamonds charlatans dishonest merchants and their associates he stepped inside turned the lock behind him hung up his coat made his way to the kitchen and moments later while fully ignoring the still surging city in frenzied neon outside the window he found a deep and all-engulfing solace in thoughts of mountainous green Pacific islands and a piping hot cup of English tea

the fundamental

ultimate insistence of the fundamental
you knew these
self-deceptions inevitably dissolve,
smoke-wisps over solid rooftops immediate
rich depth of morning coffee indescribably
intricate texture of wet
pine needles scattered rocks
hollow logs across the mud-trails empty
fruit-crates tossed into dry riverbeds
roads headlights plunging
into moon-drenched distances
persistence of the magnifying mirror's
will, such hours
in pure slumber weaving you know
these husks of electric worlds
to leap into and absolutely fill

invisible boulders

but there were still wild mountains yes ranges upon ranges all pointing
   to the golden East all still thoroughly unacknowledged in a
triumphant instant they unanimously generally with a trumpeter's
blast deemed insects crustaceans and all manner of similar creatures
         wholly unacceptable no effort of vision spared for nuisance and
folly they were making love passionately to fields of wild roses
   ejaculations of mantras of praises phrase after vociferous phrase
showering down in vast delirious excess soaking the delicate petals they
constructed altars in the forms of monuments palaces stadiums entire
         cities each thoroughly unblemished entirely devoid of visible
flaw or unintended mark and on every spotless wall a towering
painting vivid an imaginary face glowing youthful entirely free of cuts
birth marks any manner of wrinkle adorned with crowns of dark fiery
   jewels sparkling coins they put on their blindfolds dancing chanting
         singing prayers shouting praises to the giant lifeless eyes falling
suddenly on concrete writhing in hysterical sublimation pledging all
   and every allegiance at this moment boulders careening silently
down imaginary grassy slopes settling gently into soft valleys of
nothingness and just a few invisible grasshoppers crept up out of the
         sewers into a weird and alien sterile light and blocks away the
feverish ceremonies by now lasting into the summer far beyond the
   season's end pardon me mr. chairman if we might raise the question
what of the world's lamentations the lost dirges time destruction decay
         that which is forgotten that which is no *NO* don't be ridiculous
   you ludicrous fool such absurd mythologies lie far beyond relevance
meaning consideration constitute the maniacal domain of crackpots
and all manner of charlatans we are under absolutely no obligation
   whatsoever to give even the slightest conciliatory acknowledgement
indeed our selective/collective vision/attention would never dare nor
deign to endeavor to be the shameful architect of such ghastly
   grotesque and entirely unacceptable structures no never
                              nevernevernever never   never

cards

thrown that channel shake
resonate *twist* out that shouting
up at the deaf streetlamp the filthy
snow *pummeling* I'm done
pretending I'm done pretending
won't pretend again if all that
seems gives way buckles collapses
like a house of bloodstained
cards then so be the ruin
of the inevitable crushing slipping
FLOW into
one of those towns revered
for eluding the oppression of time
of a century's jackboot Hey Sam said
the ragged man on the courthouse
steps ain't seen you since
the Ice Age I think damn them
glaciers were such an awful nuisance
wouldn't you agree Sam not my
name agree Sam agree the court
compels argument of agreement forthwith
henceforth hereafter referring to the
defendant forthwith ye olden
magistrates of the magic feckless
state henceforth adorned shattered
scorned by thee and thou asunder thrown
to the disastrously haphazardly mistaken
for someone else not
pretending not contending no won't
you PLEASE
agree won't
in any way
agree the gray coast
glimpsed through thick glass smears
it all smears away now the
channel collapsing into
I could hear the
anachronistic shingles *torn*
off by the wind off out twist the filthy
weeds trash old banana peels strewn
everywhere went out shaking in the

dawn to find the shingles in
the dunes but no luck no eureka no
pot of gold not
my name no
singing sprites or leprechauns
they must have been washed
out to sea in the smoky night
while the
streetlamp heard
nothing
just stood
there
like an
idiot
and again
won't pretend
can't begin
to definitively
agree

bowler

damn these dusty doldrums we must sail OK
here we go, off we go old King Joe
with the cotton-toothed martyred banjo
shoved up your nose unknown yet knotted slow to wait no
no wait no shoddy flim-flam rationale, let's flail!
all slide, parachute to the juniper rail! Sally, fill
your little blue pail with precious dung, let's do
all but be undone, no sun of the acid
emptiness scorching, no fail, skip along our
sheltered beeswax trail tra la la la la la LA la
LA la la hold up there little missus seems like
we got a debris field, crusted beard

well hello there mustache-hat, mister hilarious
cantankerous shipyard bowler-boss of thin smoke-joke
shouting without voice-horn worn to flat artificial hat,
what elusive black cat said *hat* and gave you a
jeweled mace for our race, what conjured ghost
you toast no no next to the refuse my face refuses
your poisoned rain, this freedom once feigned, gained, remained!
no cardboard claim, no czar! let's tar and feather brown
your rotting cardboard form, to granite foam and
stone all heave, be now rightly thrown! alas, alarm,
will surely harm! OK let's go yo ho yo ho yo ha ha ha to filthy brine,
over the side the acid swine!

Nights

such delicacies, these silver whisperings

        singular spring moon, its light engulfing
    in no forge no flame yet blessed
rain, in saturation of we shall have
    forth world-wishes, imprints
of then sketches, rough charcoal reaches, the half-sonatas
of silver nights conceived only far beyond,
      as yet in thanks,
              unborn

Lens

if and only if you view it through the lens of
not trying to *say* anything. your step across
that threshold, the new air. didn't turn out
the way you thought dawning on inching
toward the old foul beast you'd swear to
never become but perhaps a world of that
however's not the worst just the pure despite
that sonic pleasure of this one moment
nevertheless imagined despite or the cause
of remembered besides how often does one
really hit the elusive balance however
anyway nevertheless see it lit anyway anew
as only a path of all its various colors and
intonations you've found by despite intuition
and pure necessity one delicious image to
enjoy without development wait only to find
the trench running thick with unforeseen
mud it'll take a river to purge of all this yes sir
it will

hail

shrapnel salads
rapidly developing realities seen
only through rusted keyholes
convex erudition unravels into strips
on the nail-littered pavement
recitative language
the photographer smashes his
wide-angle lens, sweeps the
shards into the gorge; fickle
favor, maybe it's scent
of nihilism

oh well, you can at last
be solid sure when you feel that
mountain hail across your face above
the treeline, when you remember
how often we invoke
the revered
in so many attempts
to invoke imaginary powers

scrapmetal

Whoa catch those acrobatic avocado streetcleaners match
the mandrake trombone marking vertical time silicone vantage
advantage filtered out of the mastodon linoleum daguerreotypes all
partitioned through Indiana mildewpots through Cincinnati radiance
mark witness far surge of industry ransacked the mastodon
mansions snooze full of the loose shoelaces peanut warehouses
breathing while epiphany-charged ecosystems of forging fortitudes
lie in wait, convex plates of impossible subterranean tectonics

rancid rainforests adorn scrapmetal sapphires all bronze out the
Mississippi heatbrick yikes connect that stalwart conviction said
counsel for the plaintiff council of the pacifists proclaim the
blame asunder and expertly adjacent smooth the night-chants the off
chance they pranced in the miniscule moments that anyone's
chained to the resident lean-to of questioning scars, and O would
that the trapezoid screwdriver hasten to celebrate the wasting
of cataclysms O wheel forth the epicurean racetracks ontological
mandolins all breaking multiplication in the sawtooth surf the
Roanoke colossus taps Yakima desolation down to the brazen act
of sticking your thumb out in that dusty highway through the
treeless hills a sudden no-man's-land of the collective subvision
subwhisper of a subdream's dream force of they cracked open
the dam loosed the river of sludge shattered teacups pacifiers broken
banjo strings treadmills and the like hey there's old Johnny from the
aimless days didn't know you were still kickin' around well thanks a lot
for the vote of confidence breed subdivision to springdew splinter such
assumptions right down to the limestone core, breadcrumb on the
floor wordcrumb soulcrumb the shuttlecock soars past ever-cheerful
Minnesota cantankerous Snoqualmie backslide bastion diligence
radicchio trampoline trash-swimmer halfscraps on the mudflaps
roadlitter speech sparked of these miscellany scrap-piles teetering high
in the mosquito air finally junkyards bare their truths when confronted
center of dust surging synapses, hang on—

don't
speak such time, some truths are
too sublime too abrasive for this delicate air, they might
tear it all to forlorn shreds and what would be left but void-pools on
the edge of who-knows-what on the ledge of if-we-only-knew
what but wait, even the mere suggestion, here there be ancient
and ultimately haggard
cave-dwelling questions

nines

](multitudinous overt)
diatoms risk the farm (folding
freeze) their sweltering arms all in the risking weight
of turpentine grins giggles (stretched) acr
                              oss sharking stark]fins

            well don't it Victorian
tophat Ascot eyebrows scheme to   hasten]win hence climbing
fruitblast dissonant tubs of fil
thy wine beneath Clubs (of blistered richer) Nine and Nines
of chanting chanceHearts,   ]their forlorn art
wince puffy pour]ing pouri
                        ng eyes to rub   dent mast qui
ckening and convexingly   of the]in
                                    cessantly clasp (sublime)

anotherhand   ]deal
tonnage   shrill leathered climates   ]bending]wedge
                                                    wedge

            sandpaperpeel   ](extant)

repository

can't expect to improvise
a pole vault from this toothpick
undertow in weight consideration

cancellations

blink of chance fertile machinations in
dawn-fire of the timely, the system oils, spits
out such insolent spare parts, houses
its own repository where it hurls
all these mud-caked half-articulations
of visions still-born sight-frictions for lack
of a more modern facility or method

smooth oiled wall of this
twilight trench
beyond that
beyond that but the attempt
of vertical launch to a few
weak wings, vaporous wishes
yet never a foot, fingernails
in the glimpsing inches

ten stories

choke-dust of the hairy cough square in the old room
windowless condemned but then mr. rancid fear lights
a cigar deny drown it drench him with the hose rip open
the ceiling to the askance cloud-clusters, the regardless
rain! mr. pain grins pulls out a padlock no he's a snot-nosed
sleazebag shut that disrupt shove him into the claw-footed
tub shove it in his bloodshot eye fissure fracturing right off
the rusted fire escape! force of ten stories down the
ear-splitting crash the cracked street warehouses ruptured
in chemical spills tsunamis of fluorescent toxicities slicing
surge snapping tankers suspension bridges stadiums
and the wait a minute forgotten mr. narcissistic despair raising
his disgusting dripping head snickering ridiculing so he
thinks he'll chain me right at the top of the sharp iron
spire no that's never realized deflect I'm gonna undercut
undermine underestimate this jackhammer to all hazard and
haughtiness ruptured eaten away to oblivion in the deafening
acid reality of I'm gonna squeeze till it all drains out O tectonics
O universe cast your wondrous gaze witness beneath the
gaping street the derelict subway gutted for new paint jobs
burger joints little shops inhabited by grinning old men speaking
utterly new languages selling fake flowers and decades-old
newspapers

bristle

rusted boondoggles writhe out in rustparticle paragons,
                                        aggregate sieve

gauze
divert offshoot stark scrubdust
                        metacognition

if keening urges partitioned whitehot only last, then
unless if wouldn't
                dessicate impact of trajectory syntax catharsis
                clip consistent contingency

convex fungus mother, cradle mantra:
                        institutionalized cautionary

partition hijack compounded stitch brickslash stockpile
                                        enough combustion

relegate
rhapsodic pitch-plumbing windfalls intact
        struck questionless concrete fallow amplified
        before the lash, what could marking until discernment shrill
        tenuous of a vaporous phrase

acerbic
tributary bland scofflaw seething will: the claim cantankerous, all
                                of an inching resultant

acidic pedigree
shibboleths catapult left surrogate filamentfracture

anodyne rifts convince the plethora,
                        calibrate spur of absolute thirst

yet wouldn't we claim
all such contradictions, such weighty caissons feed afterglow
                                        of the alkaline razor

but only wouldn't
we fickle flimsy fullness own that shielded albatross, a singular
                                and unmistakably forthright
                                kneecrawl

=glistening

the cop pulled up (=no
lights) gravelcrunch leisure stickyswamp ramifications
      filtered
mosquitos buzzing buzz in forthright senselessly blessings hey
did you littersneeze this sidewalk
she inquired =no way (I replied) then soon slipped
      fleas and wholly into untapped
ritual into oftentimes alternate roadsketches well she
didn't give chase nor keep pace nor wing alarms or fortnight
      warnings bye
bye the sing soon it was just all glistening
through mosquitos stickybuzz fling like =windchimes
of a thousand sundrenched
indecipherable porches

Orchards

The iron cabinet ruptures. Collapses in on itself with a shriek, spewing its volumes of old nails and empty tin cans. Skydivers hesitate. A massive monolithic office building on huge wheels, careening wildly through the astonished city streets all severe downhill angles to the inescapable harbor. Orchards produce results, accumulate. Meadows erode, acceleration. Forty broken barstools in the mezzanine, each half-painted and drowning in rivers of detergent and egg whites. The clipped yew-boughs strewn about the yard now that the higher temperatures initially accumulated in the direction of. Scripts. Until the review. Indiscriminate deaf razor chopping off rooftops and the shopkeepers shake fists complain to dead cockroaches on the mud-caked sidewalks and everywhere bellowing into the night's apprehension the wind's contradiction hurling detached mannequin's arms across fractured tennis courts over the arrogant spires of blind skyscrapers the wind's world-shaking breath pushing gargantuan sand-clouds across vast trackless reaches of ocean the unsuspecting shorelines beyond patterned responses responses are what they're trained for trained for oh yes patterns patterns as if all the world is just convenient patterns the symmetry never disrupted not a line out of place he scowls at the annoying young man making such sneering sarcastic suggestions but then all conversation abruptly stops as rich tranquility enters the room without explanation. Your unattempted question. Dropped fumbled like a lost coin down the deep mine shaft of such. A moment reluctantly. The sleep of cats, regardless. Intuition. Exploding network of a world; we destroy our homes in exchange for nothing and no certainties again. Frenzied factories churning out mindsets by the multitude, you can buy them on any corner for discount rates maybe try one for each day of the week or even every hour for the struggles of the years at last found him settled into a hard-won peace into an unusual yet comfortable self he never would have anticipated this time then every dawn he will hike up the highest ridge overlooking the lake sing of passion time of that which has eroded away that which endures and that which grows anew sing out in full voice across distance until the sun finds its peak high in the vast blue meanwhile antelopes pontificate in urban museums of glass enjoying fine cognac artichoke bundles of kale wrapped in old department-store catalogs painted jagged lightning-passions testing the mountaintops shattering the defiant glaciers suddenly every orchard supercharged exploding the rivers overflowing with vivid apples choked with bounteous apples each one luminous enchanting transcendent populations cry out convulsing with euphoria mouths foaming with transformative joy and empires erupt with disintegrating paradigms dissolving veils of haggard dissonance giving way to new singular alignments of heretofore unknown submarine depths of mind-trenches. Accumulations. Surplus of parachutes, they all abandoned the plane well before the gorge. Sextants yearn for awakenings. Events. Paths turn, not so rocky now of the rain. Now that the downpour. Results. Determinations. That which. Has yet to be determined.

www.ingramcontent.com/pod-product-compliance
Lightning Source LLC
LaVergne TN
LVHW041308080426
835510LV00009B/905